The Capture Your Neighborhood Formula--How To Get Free Advertising For Your Business

Gordon Van Wechel

The Capture Your Neighborhood Formula

Gordon Van Wechel

CONTENTS

Legal Stuff

In several places in this book I share results I have achieved in my own companies, and the results of my clients who have implemented these strategies in their businesses. You should not assume that you will have the same results. You could do better, or you could do worse...there are a lot of variables in creating and managing a marketing program.

I have updated this edition to reflect the most current information available to me. Some of the vendors I suggest you investigate may have changed their offer and/or pricing between the time I'm writing this and when you talk with them. That happens in business and is beyond my control.

Welcome!

I believe you are really going to like the marketing strategy I'm about to share with you. The Capture Your Neighborhood Formula isn't a theory. I have proven it works time and time again in my own businesses, as well as with numerous consulting clients.

I have written summary White Paper reports in the past about this marketing strategy, but for this expanded "book" edition I have included up to the minute information on how to reduce both costs and time investment by taking advantage of outsourcing service providers you can find on the Internet. I have dramatically increased my own efficiency in the past eighteen months by utilizing outsourcing, and encourage you to look into it too.

After talking with users of the CYN Formula, I've also added a section for the book with some tips on how to write effective ad copy for your campaigns. This is by no means an exhaustive lesson on copywriting, but I want to share some basics that have been helpful to my consulting clients.

One other comment before we begin. I decided to start this book with a chapter that is not directly related to the Capture Your Neighborhood Formula, but is a critically important concept for any business owner to know. That is what I call "The Basic Equation of Business." This is a concept that I often demonstrate when speaking to a group of business owners and always review with my consulting clients. I hope you find it useful too.

There is no single marketing program that fits every company, nor should any business owner rely on one strategy for business growth in today's highly competitive market. However, after more than 25 years of starting and growing my own companies, and the last 11 years as a business growth consultant, I believe that the Capture Your Neighborhood Formula is the single best and most cost efficient way to grow a business on a limited marketing budget.

I encourage you to consider using the Capture Your Neighborhood Formula as one of the tools for growing your business.

To Your Success!

Gordon

CHAPTER ONE

LITTLE HINGES SWING BIG DOORS: THE BASIC EQUATION OF BUSINESS

The statistics are startling. Over 50% of the new businesses that are started in the United States fail within the first two years. More than 80% don't survive until their 5th birthday,

Why do you suppose that is?

Well meaning budding entrepreneurs will make an "all in" bet on their venture. They'll mortgage their home, cash in retirement accounts, and borrow from relatives to get the doors open. That's when the real work begins. For the most part, the new business owner is a hard worker, wearing multiple hats as he or she attempts to become successful.

But the overwhelming majority of these hopeful business people fail. Why?

In my conversations with hundreds of business owners over the years that I have been a consultant, eleven at the time I'm writing this, I see two primary causes for failure. First, not being crystal clear on what they want to accomplish, and second, not understanding the "Basic Equation of Business." The first one is something that cannot be fixed by reading a book. The second though, is very correctable once you understand how it works.

The "Basic Equation" is the name I use to describe the complete flow of a business from the very beginning, finding a lead; right through to the end: you as the owner putting profits into your pocket. I first heard this concept in a presentation by Australian businessman Brad Sugars. He was speaking at a conference I attended in Las Vegas and talked about the "business chassis." The following day I was fortunate to be seated at his table for a luncheon, and he elaborated on the idea. I don't know or understand cars, so I've changed the metaphor a bit, but the essence of the equation is the same.

In this chapter I'm going to first share with you the components of the equation, then give you some examples of how it works in a real business with real numbers. I firmly believe, and this has been proven with my own clients, that once you understand the Basic Equation of Business you will never look at your own enterprise the same way again.

I think it was Dan Kennedy who said that, "little hinges swing big doors." That is really the concept I want to share with you in this opening chapter. Once you understand the Basic Equation you will have the power to effect big swings for your company.

Let me first list the components of the equation and their relationship, then I'll elaborate on each one of them. For those of you who labor under the mistaken notion that "my business is different" and assume this doesn't apply to you...well, you're wrong! Whether you manufacture widgets or sell ice cream or help people out of their legal problems-- this equation applies to your business. So open your mind and see how understanding can lead to more profits. After all, isn't that why you have a business?

The Basic Equation has eight components. I'll list them, as well as put the "operator" in between each component so you can see how they work together.

1. **Leads** (prospects or potential customers)

Multiplied by

2. **Conversion Rate** (the difference between those that could have bought and those that did)

Equals

3. **Customers** (the total number of different customers you deal with)

Multiplied by

4. **Number of Transactions** (the average number of times each customer buys in a year)

Multiplied by

5. **Average Dollar Sale Price** (the average price of the items you sell)

Equals

6. **Sales** (the total amount of business done in a given time period)

Multiplied by

7. **Margins** (the percentage of each sale that is profit)

Equals

8. **Profit** (the reason you own your business and work so hard)

Now that you've seen the Equation, let's further define each component.

Your Number of Leads--the total number of potential buyers that you contacted or that contacted you in the last year (or whatever increment of time you want to measure). Most business people confuse responses, the number of potential buyers, with results. Just because the phone is ringing doesn't mean the cash register is.

What is even more surprising is the reality that very few businesses have an idea how many leads they actually get in a week, let alone have a method for determining the specific marketing campaign that they came from. It's a good thing to get a lot of leads, but then you've got to remember your...

Conversion Rate--The percentage of people who did buy as opposed to those who inquired. For example, if you had ten people walk into your store today but only four purchased anything, then you have a conversion rate of 4 out of 10, or 40%. This is, for most businesses, the fastest and easiest way to increase profits. You already have someone interested in your product or service, now you just have to get them to take the last step and buy.

When I have this conversation with most business owners, they have no idea what their conversion rate really is. Typically they will guess high--like 60%. Then when we actually put some metrics in place and measure, the result is more like 20%. This might seem disappointing, but it's really a blessing in disguise. Imagine how your business will run when the conversion rate is increased to 40%, or even higher. If you double your conversion rate you double your profit!

Number of Customers--This is the total number of different customers you deal with in a period of time. It is the product of the number of leads times your conversion rate. Most business owners who do not understand the Basic Equation can be heard saying, "oh, if I only had more customers." That says they haven't yet realized how business works. The number of customers is a result, not a variable. To increase you customer count you need more leads and/or a higher conversion rate.

Number of Transactions--This is another of the five variables in the equation. Some customers will buy from you frequently, other just occasionally, and still others just once in a lifetime. The number you are trying to determine here is the average number of times a customer buys from you in a year. Don't consider just the best customers, or the worst-- it's the average that is important.

This is another place in the equation where an incremental change can have a huge impact on profits. In today's business environment it is a simple exercise to collect a database of customers. Most owners do not take the time to do this. Big Mistake! A simple postcard, phone call, even an email inviting them to come back will yield big profits.

Average Dollar Sale--This is a number that most business owners are familiar with. It's a simple calculation: take your total sales and divide by the number of sales made.

Sales--This is another multiplication problem. Multiply the total number of customers by the average number of times they shop with you, and then by the average amount they spend. That result is your sales, sometimes called "turnover." Most owners will have an idea about turnover, often relating it to how many times a year they "turn over" their inventory. That's thinking in the right direction, but doesn't fully grasp the idea of this number, how it is calculated, or most important, how to impact this figure.

Margins--The percentage of each and every sale that is profit. This is likely going to be different for each product or service you sell, but the calculation is easy. If you sell something for $100 and after all the costs of your business are taken out you have $10 left over, then you have a 10% margin.

Profit--Of course another result that we all want more of. Once again, you cannot directly get more profit. What you can do is increase your margin on the sales you have.

So there you have it--the Basic Equation of Business in all its glorious simplicity. This equation is the model that determines the profit level of every business on earth.

Once you realize that by analyzing your business using this equation, and focusing your attention on the five variables that you can control, you are ahead of the vast majority of business owners in the marketplace.

To prove beyond a reasonable doubt the power of this formula let's put some numbers into the equation, and then do some simple "what if" scenarios. Here we go:

1. Leads: 1000

Multiplied by

2. Conversion Rate: 25%

Equals

3. Customers: 250

Multiplied by

4. Number of Transactions: 2

Multiplied by

5. Average Dollar Sale Price: $100

Equals

6. Sales: $50,000

Multiplied by

7. Margin: 25%

Equals

8. Profit: $12,500

Now let's have some fun. What happens when you can increase each of the variables by just 10%? Logic says your profit should increase by 10% too, right? Get your calculator and check my math:

1. **Leads: 1100**

Multiplied by

2. **Conversion Rate: 27.5%**

Equals

3. **Customers: 302**

Multiplied by

4. **Number of Transactions: 2.2**

Multiplied by

5. **Average Dollar Sale Price: $110**

Equals

6. **Sales: $73,084**

Multiplied by

7. **Margin: 27.5%**

Equals

8. **Profit: $20,098**

WOW! Profit didn't increase by 10%, more like over 60%! Just by adding a 10% improvement in each of the variables you increase your profits by over 60%.

Shall we do one more? Let's assume that, over a period of time and with diligent work, you could double each of the variables. Again, logic would dictate that your profits would double…but I don't think I can fool with that one again. So let's check and see how the numbers work out (grab your calculator!)

Here's what happens when you DOUBLE the variables:

1. Leads: 2000

Multiplied by

2. Conversion Rate: 50%

Equals

3. Customers: 1000

Multiplied by

4. Number of Transactions: 4

Multiplied by

5. Average Dollar Sale Price: $200

Equals

6. Sales: $80,000

Multiplied by

7. Margin: 50%

Equals

8. Profit: $40,000

Your immediate reaction might be, "that's a silly example. It is unrealistic to think you can double each of the variables." But is it? The Japanese have a word, 'Kaizen'. It's a word they use to describe the effort to always be improving your results. In fact, the literal translation is "constant improvement."

Apply Kaizen to your business. What if you were able to improve each of the variables by just 1% a week, or even just 1% a month. Where would you be in a year? In five years? You've already committed your time and energy to the business, what about focusing on incremental changes in each of these areas?

Of course that sounds good, but how to do it is the million dollar question. In this book I'm going to share how to implement just one strategy, the Capture Your Neighborhood Formula. There are many more ways we teach that will help you increase your business profitability over time. At the end of the book I'll give you some information about our company, and if you're interested, offer you a valuable free consultation.

Remember, little hinges swing big doors!

CHAPTER TWO

HOW IT ALL BEGAN

As some of you know, I have started and built three national companies in three distinct industries. One of those was a mortgage company. A friend from college and I were working for another company in that industry trying to "learn the business." When we felt we were ready, we made the decision to launch our own venture.

I borrowed $5000 from my father to fund the enterprise. Most of that went for a software program that enabled us to process loan applications and manage a loan pipeline (yes, we were optimistic!) We paid the first two months rent on a 150 square foot "executive suite" that included furniture and a telephone receptionist. We couldn't afford to buy new computers, so we moved our personal computers from home into the space, as well as a Mr. Coffee machine so we could 'brew our own.'

It was with a certain amount of satisfaction that we came into our new empire that first Monday and were enjoying a cup of coffee together. Until Andy asked the relevant question: "OK, we're here and set up...where are we going to get some loan business?"

As the 'leader' of our team, I had done what so many other budding entrepreneurs before me have done. Gotten all excited about a business idea, planned and built infrastructure, opened the doors--but had not considered how I was going to attract customers. We were essentially out of money, having run through the seed capital from Dad. It typically takes anywhere from three to six weeks to process and close a loan, so even if we had a new customer that very day, we wouldn't get paid for a month or more.

This required some quick thinking!

The traditional ways of getting loans, working with Realtors, required months to build relationships based on trust before they'd give you a chance with one of their clients. We couldn't wait that long. We were in a strong refinance market at that time, so I knew that was our fastest path to cash. But how to find a homeowner who was interested in talking about a new mortgage loan? That was the challenge.

I had a friend who owned a couple of carpet cleaning trucks. Tom and I had been talking a couple of weeks earlier about how he wanted to add another truck and crew and expand into some new parts of town. I got an idea, did some quick research, and gave Tom a call.

"Tom," I said, "how would you like to partner with Andy and I on a marketing campaign into the Greenwood Village neighborhoods." This was a moderately upscale part of town, not wealthy homeowners but a solid family area with good schools and upper mid-level income residents.

Tom wanted to know more.

"Why don't we go in together on a postcard and mail it to every home in the area. Because it's coming in the mail it will have a better chance of getting noticed than hiring one of the flyer companies to go door to door, and we can each take half of the card and share the cost."

Tom agreed, with the stipulation that he didn't have any time to work on this, he'd pay his share as long as I did all the work to make it happen. "Exactly what I had in mind!" was my quick response.

Long story short, I had found a new "Quick Press" printer who was willing to do a job at cost for the right to all of our future business. His daughter did the layout for free, and in a few days we hit the post office with 1000 full color postcards. They were about 5 inches by 7 inches, with an ad for each of our companies on the front, and some copy about "we are in the neighborhood" on the back. I still remember the total cost of the project: $438.72. I gave Tom that total, and he wrote a check on the spot. "If this works well," he said, "let's do some more. That's pretty cheap advertising."

As I recall, Tom got 14 or 15 jobs from that little mailing, and we did do more of these joint efforts over the years. Andy and I got 7 calls and did two loans. We closed them within a month, reinvested the profits, and began to grow our company. Five years later we were doing business in 38 states, had over 100 employees, and did $60 million in business.

Hard to believe it all started with a postcard!

Fast Forward to Today

For the past eleven years I have worked as a business growth consultant. That position has given me the opportunity to work with companies in many sectors. From small retail shops to multi-state distribution companies, professional practices to financial services firms. In all cases the business owners face the same challenge that Andy and I did many years ago: how to attract new prospects and help them become customers.

I almost always suggest the Capture Your Neighborhood Formula as one of the off-line strategies they should implement. It meets all three of the important criteria I have for a business growth strategy:

- ✓ It is easy to do, and can be delegated to a team member
- ✓ It is low cost...like $0 cost to you in most cases
- ✓ IT WORKS!

With the emphasis today on Internet marketing and the frenzy over Social Media, "old school" ideas like direct mail often get shoved aside as archaic. Yet, dollar for dollar, I consistently see better results, and more trackable results, from the mail than the world wide web. That doesn't apply to all situations and all businesses, but in most cases is true. And if you implement the Capture Your Neighborhood Formula as I teach it, you will have massive amounts of marketing leverage with a minimum of risk.

Here's the bottom line: if I were to be dropped into a strange city in a state that I had never visited, and told to start a successful business from scratch quickly, the Capture Your Neighborhood Formula is exactly what I'd use. Welcome to a "new/old" world of marketing innovation! So let's get into it!

CHAPTER THREE

THE CAPTURE YOUR NEIGHBORHOOD FORMULA

In one simple sentence, here is the formula:

Identify two non-competing businesses that want to target the same group of prospects that you do, combine their offers with yours on a large postcard, and mail thousands of them.

What makes this so powerful is that if you use the right resources and structure the deal correctly, one of the three ads can be free. Stop and think about that. If the third section of the postcard is your business, you are accessing the power of a large, targeted direct mail campaign *without paying anything!*

Think that sounds too good to be true? I'm going to show you how to routinely get the cost of the mailing, including postage, to less than 75 cents per card, frequently as low as 60 cents. So that means you need to get less than 40 cents from each of the other participants and your space is FREE. How many business people do you know right now who would jump on the idea of sending a large, full color printed on both sides postcard, to a targeted group of their prospects, for something under 40 cents? Especially if they didn't have to do any of the work! You should know a lot of them.

Today's Marketing Environment

If you're a small business owner struggling to grow your company I know you get a ton of phone calls promising to get you on the front page of Google or make you a hero on Facebook. That doesn't begin to consider the companies who want to redesign your website or create a social media campaign for you. It seems like every 25 year old with a computer is an Internet Marketing Guru.

As the web has taken the spotlight, more traditional marketing venues have lost market share and become more expensive. Have you priced a display ad in your local newspaper lately? Ad costs are up over 40% in the last couple of years in most cities with a daily paper.

Radio ads? Almost as much of a price increase. Plus you need to run dozens of spots over time to get the awareness penetration you'll need to generate customers.

The Yellow Pages have been replaced by the "online Yellow Pages." Same concept, just pixels instead of paper. If many of your customers are over 40 years of age, they may not be as comfortable using the computer and never see your ads.

Telemarketing? That's a quick way to make your prospects mad.

Trade shows? Really difficult for a local business to absorb the expense for a booth plus the cost of creating a display and the give-aways you'd need. Plus the staff cost to have people in the booth.

Direct Mail is for most small business owners the most cost effective way to reach a targeted group of prospects. Plus, if you properly structure your offer, you will be able to measure the results of your campaign and calculate an accurate return on your marketing investment. That's tough to do on the internet.

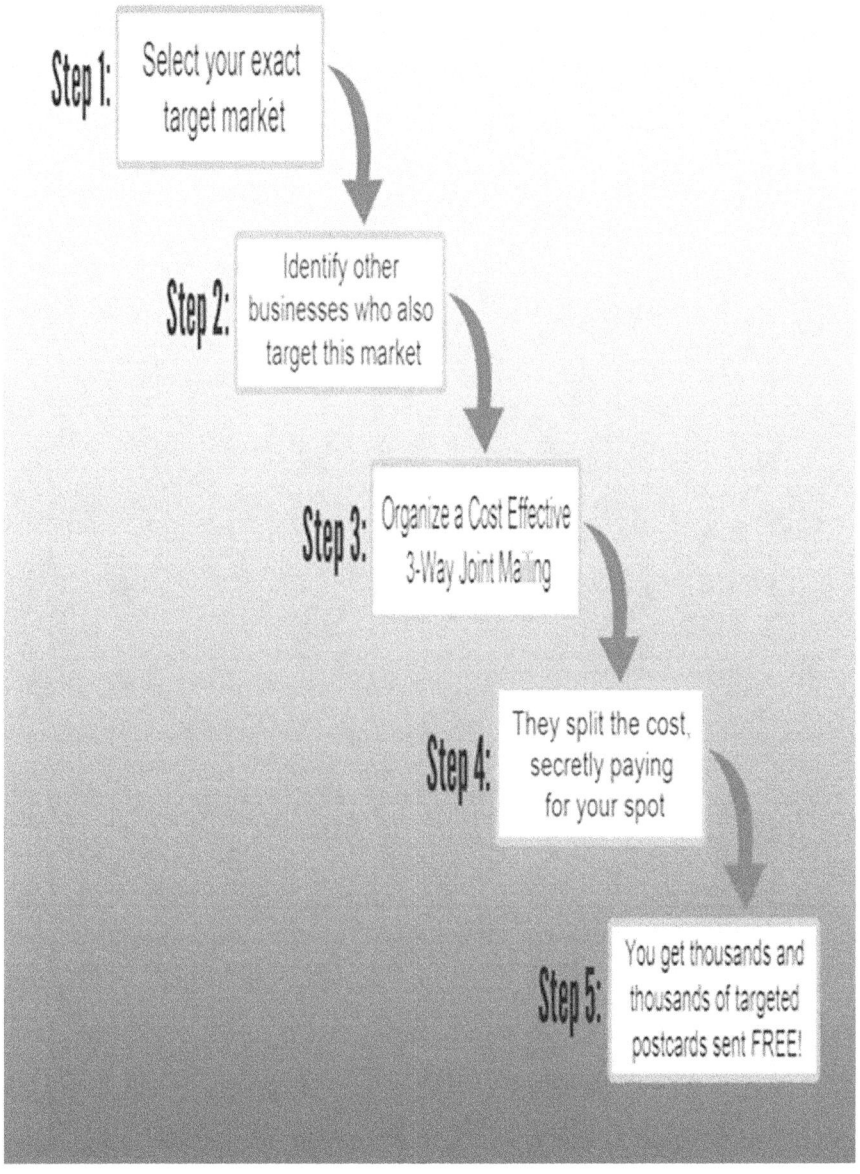

Gordon Van Wechel

CHAPTER FOUR

HOW TO IMPLEMENT THE CAPTURE YOUR NEIGHBORHOOD FORMULA

The key to making the Capture Your Neighborhood Formula work is carefully determining who you are targeting. The formula works whether you are targeting business to business or business to consumer. Let's talk about business to business first. Here's an example:

Assume you are in the credit card processing business, and your company has just introduced a new program that can save retail clothing and shoe stores 25% of the normal fee each month if they switch their processing account to you. This is a great deal, and you want to get it in front of as many shop owners as possible, and quickly.

The first step is to identify your target market. There are a variety of ways to do this, I'll give you some in a later chapter. For the purpose of this example, let's say you live in Denver, and identified 1780 businesses that fit your search criteria in the metro area.

One important fact to remember when mailing to businesses. You want to send to companies that are small enough that the owner is likely to read the mail themselves. Sending postcards to corporate outlets is not going to be as effective. So in this example, I would not mail to the local mall shoe store that is part of a national chain.

Second, think of who else wants to target retail clothing and shoe stores? Some immediate examples would include:

- ✓ Janitorial companies
- ✓ Payroll services
- ✓ Accounting and bookkeeping services
- ✓ Office supply
- ✓ Insurance agents
- ✓ Carpet cleaners
- ✓ Window washers
- ✓ Delivery services
- ✓ Phone system companies
- ✓ 'Mr. Fix-it' carpenter or electrician
- ✓ Deli or sandwich shops that deliver

In fact, this list I've just given you would be interested in almost any small business target group you might identify. I'm sure that if you think for a few minutes, or do a little Google market research, you will be able to come up with several more likely target categories.

As you think about these companies you will probably be able to identify sub-categories for many of them. Which is to say that it is not uncommon to create a list of 35 to 50 potential partner categories for any target market. And who knows how many individual companies within each category?

Remember, you only need two of these companies to get a Capture Your Neighborhood campaign started!

Step three is to begin contacting these companies with your offer to joint venture a marketing campaign with you. I'll give you some scripts in a minute.

If you are apprehensive about the "selling" aspect of the CYN Formula let me put your mind at ease. This is not like cold calling or the typical prospecting you may have done at some time in your career. There is an essential difference here. You are not approaching them as a salesperson hoping for an opportunity. Instead, you are a business owner talking with another business owner about working together to grow your respective companies. It is a completely different dynamic.

Finally, once you have your two partners for the project, you handle the fulfillment. That is, you coordinate helping your new "advertising partners" with their ads. That means getting their logo or other artwork, taking their copy and having your layout person design the postcard. I always like to print a copy of the final layout and have them review before going to the printer. You will also coordinate the mailing list and getting the cards into the mail.

Before you say, "I don't have time to do all of that" let me assure you it is easy. After you do the first campaign, you'll be able to have someone on your team do all of this. The key is getting other business owners to join you, the mechanics of putting the postcards together and getting them mailed is a straightforward exercise.

Business to Consumer campaigns are handled exactly the same way. The difference is in the target market. Instead of a list of companies all over town, you'll be targeting a neighborhood of homeowners. This is actually easier. The Every Door Direct Mail service from the US Post Office has both lowered the cost of mailing and simplified the targeting. (More on this relatively new service later.)

The pool of joint venture partners who are looking for homeowner leads is larger, and easier to work with. Just think for a minute about all the businesses who work directly with consumers:

Home Services:

- ✓ Roofing
- ✓ Pest Control
- ✓ Plumber
- ✓ HVAC
- ✓ Pool Service
- ✓ Window/Door/Insulation
- ✓ Driveway and Paving
- ✓ House Cleaning
- ✓ Carpet Cleaning

Professional Services:

- ✓ Furniture Store
- ✓ Appliance Store
- ✓ Interior Design
- ✓ Luxury Car Dealer
- ✓ Home Equity Lender
- ✓ Realtors
- ✓ Home Health Care provider

In most cities you can find at least five companies for each of these categories. So the supply of potential joint venture partners is huge.

Prospecting For Marketing Partners

You can use a variety of ways to get your message to a potential marketing partner. Here are a few:

- ✓ email (this will usually be a cold contact)
- ✓ cold calling by phone
- ✓ networking
- ✓ personal face to face call
- ✓ voice broadcasting technology (more on this later)

All of these methods work well with the CYN Formula. Try them and see which is the most efficient for you.

So what do you say when you make contact? Here's an example of a script that will work for any of the techniques I just mentioned except for voice broadcasting. I'll give you the script, and then analyze it for you. I'll continue to use the example of the credit card services company, and I'm writing to an insurance agent. See what you think:

Hello,

I think you're really going to like this.

My name is Gordon Van Wechel, and I'm currently getting ready to send a direct mailing out to local clothing and shoe stores throughout Denver (there's about 1780 of them!) I sell credit card processing services to them and direct mail usually gets about a 2% response for me (30 to 40 new clients).

I'm sure that there's a lot of clothing and shoe stores in Denver that could use a review of their business insurance, so I thought you could use some more clients as well. If you want to share the mailing with me and another business that doesn't compete, we can split the cost up for ridiculously cheap. If we use a large 6x11 postcard, it leaves a ton of space for each of us on the front and back in full glossy color.

Let me know if you're interested. I'd like to have you rather than another insurance agent on it, but I've got to know so I can get this going right away.

Thank you.

Gordon
(contact info)

Here is why I have phrased the copy as I have. Remember, this approach works for an email, telephone script, and the outline of a personal conversation. You want to be sure to get these points into your presentation regardless of how you get in front of them:

- identify the specific size of the mailing, it shows you've done your homework
- give a small percentage response rate, but more important translate that into *number of clients*
- be upbeat, positive that the mailing is going to be productive
- use curiosity seeking phrases like "ridiculously cheap" that will frame their response when they ask how much that is
- use scarcity or fear of loss by mentioning you'll get one of their competitors if they don't respond quickly

The typical response from the prospect is going to be asking about the cost. This is good, it means they are interested and open to doing a joint venture with you. Here is how I reply:

> *John, I'm really glad you're interested. I've been frustrated with advertising so many times, and have found that the mail works best by far.*

> *I'm fortunate to have a good friend who runs a print and mail shop, so I'm able to get things done really inexpensively. The biggest postcard we can send affordably through the mail is 6x11, which is an enormous size. We can do it on thick card stock with glossy coating and full color on both sides.*

The mailing list, mailing preparation, printing, and postage to 1780 local clothing and shoe stores comes out to 69 cents each. So if we split this three ways it works out to just 23 cents for each of us. I'd like to send more, but personally I can't handle too many new clients at one time so I just want to do 1780 at the moment, if that's OK with you John.

Gordon

Here's some key factors:

- use their name, it's good to get personal
- be assumptive, act as if they're ready to do this
- reinforce that the mail has worked better than other marketing
- an itemized description of all that is involved so that the price makes logical sense
- when quoting the price breakdown, use the per piece cost, not the total dollar investment

Is the approach different when looking for Business to Consumer joint venture partners? No, not really. Here's how I'd modify the first email to reflect the approach to homeowners. For this example, I'll pretend I'm in the granite countertop business, and I'm contacting a carpet cleaner.

Hello,

I'm with New Era Granite Countertops here in South Denver and I'm doing another postcard mailing to homeowners here in Denver that make over $100,000 annually (I have a targeted list.)

I figure that if I can share an even bigger full color

postcard (6x11) with another local guy who wants the same clientele, we can get twice the mailing, or cut the cost in half. Even better if 3 of us do it, I'm willing to do any amount up to 5,000 mailings because it'll be so cheap.

I can't send more than that right now because even 1% (50 new leads) will be more than we can handle at the moment, but I know this is a better way to get leads than anything else out there. I might as well share it with some local guys who don't compete with me, like you.

Let me know so I don't have to look for another carpet cleaning company.

Gordon
(contact info)

I could just as easily have been promoting a mailing to a neighborhood by name, or one or more carrier routes as you will do when using Every Door Direct Mail. The approach is the same, as is the follow up. Your goal is to find just two joint venture mailing partners for each campaign, partners who do not compete with you, but who also have a vested interest in the same group of prospects.

CHAPTER FIVE

EXPANDING THE CAPTURE YOUR NEIGHBORHOOD FORMULA

Let's do a quick summary of what we've learned so far.

The Capture Your Neighborhood Formula is nothing more than identifying two non-competing businesses that want to target the same group of prospects, combining their offers on a large postcard, and mailing thousands of them.

To accomplish this you follow a four step process:

1. Identify your target market.

2. Think of other companies who target the same audience.

3. Contact those business owners and arrange a cost effective three way joint mailing

4. Manage the production and mailing of the post cards, sending thousands of cards targeted to your market for FREE.

If there is a place in the process where I've seen my consulting clients get hung up, at least as they begin to implement the CYN Formula, it's in the prospecting...contacting other business owners and sharing the opportunity with them. To help with that I've given you some proven scripts that should convert for you with just a little practice.

There are two more important pieces of information I want to make you aware of. First, some ideas about how to scale the Formula, both for your own business and for others. Second, a list of resources that will help you manage the fulfillment part of the program easily and with a minimum of expense. So let's jump into those.

Capture Your Neighborhood on Steroids

I hope by now you've realized how powerful the marketing leverage of the CYN Formula can be. You might begin with a single campaign to 1000 homes or businesses. But with just a few additional phone calls you could find two partners for a second mailing. This might go to the same 1000 homes or businesses (doubling your touches to this group, still at little or no cost) or a completely new market.

What is so great about CYN is that you can choose to whom and how often you market. You can test offers to your prospects to find those that convert the best--all while using other people's money. It is not uncommon for business owners to whom I've taught this system to have multiple partnerships working at the same time, with 40,000 or more pieces going to their target market each month, at no cost to them other than the time to manage the program.

Let's talk about that. I know you have a business to run, and if you're like most business owners you already have too many responsibilities and not enough time as it is. The last thing you need is another "job" to do. Again, that is one of the beauties of the CYN Formula, it can easily be delegated.

Once you've identified the best fulfillment partners (suggestions on these coming up) the actual preparation of the postcards, printing, and mailing become a simple series of actions that can be readily taught to a staff person. Your job is primarily talking with other business owners and putting the partnerships together.

Even this becomes easy after just a few months. What you'll find is that your partners keep coming back to you asking when the next mailing is scheduled, and can they get in? Once they've seen the results from their postcards they'll want to continue, and appreciate you taking charge and making it happen. So even the prospecting activity becomes minimal after the first few mailings.

Perhaps the most successful person I have worked with who uses CYN is a Realtor in Dallas. Alex came to my consulting firm looking for ways to increase his business. He had already implemented a "team approach," having several other agent 'specialists' that he managed. We helped him do a few things to his website and social media presence, but he really wanted to expand into some of the newer and more expensive neighborhoods in his city and the internet was just not accomplishing that for him.

We taught him the Capture Your Neighborhood Formula, and helped him get his first mailing assembled. He liked the results so much that he soon had put together three additional partnerships and was mailing each month. He then trained one of his assistants to handle the entire program. Last time I talked with Alex he had an average of 90,000 postcards a month being sent through between five and fifteen partnerships. His business was on every card, and his total cost each month was less than $2500, and the majority of that expense was for his staff person who spent most of her time on this program. If you do the math, that's less than 3 cents per postcard!

Capture Your Neighborhood as a Profit Center

My Realtor friend Alex uses CYN to promote his own business, and quite successfully. With his trained assistant, he could just as easily use CYN as a lead generation platform and broker partnerships for a profit. Here's what I mean.

Let's say you identify a list of homeowners in a neighborhood that is fifteen years old, all of whom earn over $100,000 each year. Homes that age are beginning to need some sprucing up, and many of the owners are in an economic position to be able to consider that. What if you were to put together a postcard joint venture with three businesses that would like to target that group--maybe an interior designer, a kitchen/bath remodeling company, and an upscale floor coverings company? You negotiate a referral fee with each of them that could be just a flat fee for each lead, or perhaps a lead fee and a percentage of the job they sell.

Your assistant sets up the postcards and manages the mailing. You have almost no time invested in the project, but can make a profit three ways...yes, three! First, the lead referral fee, second the percentage you negotiated. The third income source is the mailing itself. Instead of charging two partners the cost of mailing and sending yours for free, you charge all three the same price, but one of the fees is your profit. So a $5000 mailing cost actually generates three fees of $2500, giving you a nice profit for your time invested.

Again, most business owners reading this book are not in a position right now to do this. But I want you to be thinking about future possibilities as you begin to do your first CYN programs.

Here are some other ideas for how to use the CYN Formula:

- ✓ Help a friend or family member with their struggling business
- ✓ Jump start a new business quickly
- ✓ Take a new idea and turn it into a profitable business
- ✓ Use CYN to raise money for a non-profit you support
- ✓ Teach a non-competing business the formula and charge a consulting fee
- ✓ Grab market share from competitors without their realizing it
- ✓ Announcements to the neighborhood for your church or service club

The Capture Your Neighborhood Formula

CHAPTER SIX

FULFILLMENT: MANAGING THE LOGISTICS OF CAPTURE YOUR NEIGHBORHOOD

Now that you understand the concept of CYN, and how to share it with potential joint venture partners, how does all the fulfillment get done? How do you actually do a direct mail campaign? With the internet, innovations in printing, and the EDDM program; this has become much easier. Fortunately, most business owners believe this is quite complicated and will be glad you are willing to do it. In fact, that will be one of the main reasons they're excited to join with you.

Let's talk first about mail processing. I've given you examples earlier in this report showing the two general types of mailings: targeted and saturation. A targeted mailing would be like the 1780 clothing and shoe stores in Denver that our credit card processing person was interested in prospecting. A saturation mailing is like Andy and I did back when we were starting our mortgage company; mailing to every homeowner in a neighborhood.

In summary then, a targeted mailing is to a list of your ideal prospects. A saturation mailing blankets entire areas, neighborhoods, or carrier routes. As a general rule, and to keep things both simple and time efficient for you, a targeted mailing should be processed by a mailing house. A saturated mailing can be done through the EDDM program at the post office or you can handle them yourself if you want to. Saturated mailings done in this way will not require expensive mailing software or permits.

Categories of Mail

For the Capture Your Neighborhood Formula we'll use postcards exclusively. I believe this is the most economical type of direct marketing for a couple of reasons. One, it is less expensive to create a mailing of a postcard campaign than to prepare a traditional direct mail piece sent in an envelope. Second (and more important) there is not an open rate to contend with, the postcard simply gets noticed and read when the recipient goes through their mail. Third, you can produce them in various sizes, make them bright and colorful, glossy--in short, they capture attention.

Postcard sizes can be confusing, especially with the standard nomenclature the post office uses. You may think that a mail piece is a "postcard," because it is a single sheet of paper. But to qualify for mailing at the First-Class Mail postcard price, it must be:

- Rectangular
- At least 3-1/2 inches high x 5 inches long x 0.007 inch thick
- No more than 4-1/4 inches high x 6 inches long x 0.016 inches thick

If a mail piece does not meet the dimensions above, then the Postal Service considers it a letter and letter-size postage is charged. With Standard Mail, there is a little more flexibility -- there is no separate (lower) price for postcards, so you don't have to worry about your postcard being too big -- because you're paying letter prices anyway.

Common "letter rate postcard" sizes are:

- 5.5 x 8.5
- 6 x 9

- 6 x 11

I always use the 6 x 11 size since they can easily fit three ads, and both sides can be used.

A postcard larger than 6-1/8" x 11-1/2" x 1/4" thick is called a "flat" and you'll have to pay flats (large envelope) postage prices. Typical sizes here are:

- 6.5 x 9
- 6.5 x 11
- 8.5 x 11
- 9 x 12

I have not found that the incremental increased size is worth the additional cost. Stick with the 6 x 11 size.

Postage

Postage costs decrease when you send in bulk with a permit and have your mailing presorted into the mail carriers walk sequence. A mail house will do all of this for you, which is why you should consider this alternative when doing a targeted mailing.

Another category of mail that is not commonly used by most of us is called Commercial Standard Mail. This is mail that has been processed prior to delivery to the post office. This processing can include various levels of sorting by carrier route as well as a bar code put on each piece to facilitate rapid processing by post office machines. This can bring the cost of each piece of mail down to a range of between 19 cents to 30 cents, depending on the level of processing. Using Commercial Standard Mail is an important part of reducing the cost of a CYN campaign, enabling you to leverage the mailing campaign to your benefit.

For saturation mailings (every address in an area receives

your postcard) the USPS has introduced a wonderful program called Every Door Direct Mail (EDDM). This has made a saturation mailing extremely simple to do without a mailing house. Here again though, there are service companies who will help you and that should be compared to the cost of your personal time spent preparing a mailing.

With a saturation mailing you can select the specific carrier routes you want your postcards delivered to. A carrier route can have between 300 and 600 addresses and may include homes, businesses, and PO boxes. If you'd like to check out carrier routes in your area you can go to: https://eddm.usps.com/eddm/customer/routeSearch.action

To take advantage of the EDDM system you must use flat, sized pieces. Acceptable sizes include 6.5 x 9, 6.5 x 11, 8.5 x 11, 9 x 12, and 12 x 15. When you meet the guidelines, EEDM mail only costs 14.5 cents per piece! You don't need a mail permit, but there are some handling requirements you must meet to earn this low cost.

First, you'll need to take physical delivery of the postcards and sort by carrier routes they'll be going to. Then the postcards need to be bundled in packages of 100 cards each, shrink wrap is a good way to keep them straight. Then they have to be delivered to the local post office that manages the specific carrier route you are mailing to.

Here's the good news about all of this. There are companies who will handle the entire process for you, including printing, sorting, wrapping, and delivering; for a very nominal fee. I'll suggest some of these in just a minute.

CHAPTER SEVEN

HOW TO IDENTIFY PROSPECTS

Remember our example of the credit card processing sales person in Denver? She wanted to target 'non-national chain' clothing and shoe stores, and developed a list of 1780 of them. How did she do that?

Well, there are quite a number of ways. Let me suggest some that I have used:

1. List Brokers. A list broker has access to massive databases that can be sorted in a seemingly infinite numbers of ways. Want to target women living in Seattle, who are stay at home moms, have a college degree, registered Republican in the last election, live in a home worth more than $400,000, and drive an automobile that is two years old or less? A good list broker can give you the names of women who meet that criteria, as well as their address and phone number, even an email address for some of them.

Finding a list broker is easy, you can Google "list broker" and find numerous national and regional companies. Do not feel like you must have a broker in your local market to get good data. The cost of using a list broker varies, but you should expect to pay a flat amount per each thousand records they find for you. That amount might be as low as $30, but could climb to several hundred dollars per thousand names for certain searches. In almost all cases you will pay for a minimum number of names, often 5000 or more, regardless of how many you need.

Something else to negotiate if you purchase a list from a

broker is how many times you can use the data. Most lists are rented, not sold, and allow a single mailing only. This can be negotiated to multiple uses, but will cost more per thousand names. Don't make the mistake of thinking you can re-mail the list and not tell the broker. All brokers "seed" their lists with a few dummy names and addresses that they control. If they get a second postcard to one of those address when you have not paid for multiple use they will bill you, and also add your name to a list of cheaters that is shared with other list brokers.

2. InfoUSA. www.infousa.com. This is one of the largest data compiling companies in America. They collect data from numerous sources, have a staff that does a telephone verification with each company in their business listings quarterly, and allows access to their data using several different plans.

You might remember a few years ago being able to purchase CD's of business listings across the country at Office Depot or Staples? Those were created by InfoUSA. Today you can access their database of more than 14 million business and 200+ million consumers from you own computer. They offer specialized lists (medical specialists, gardeners, people who attend church, etc) as well as geographical searches. Almost any kind of data sort that you can think of can be selected from their database.

You can purchase a one-time only search, or buy a subscription and be able to access the database any time you want. There are limits to how many records you can download in a month, but you can always pay a per record surcharge if you need more. The plans change frequently, so go to their website if you want to know what the current offers are.

I have personally used InfoUSA for more than 15 years with good success. Their data is accurate, and customer service is good.

3. Infofree. www.infofree.com. This is a company almost exactly like InfoUSA. In fact, the man who first started InfoUSA sold it several years ago, waited out his non-compete time, and then jumped back into the industry with Infofree.

When Infofree first started, they had a plan offering unlimited downloads for just $50 a month. That was a great deal! In the Spring of 2013 they stopped that plan and the last time I checked they now offer up to 1000 records each month for $50, and 8 cents per record if you want more.

I have also used Infofree. My experience is that their database is not as complete, that is it does not offer as many specialized search criteria as InfoUSA. Their customer service team is very responsive, almost to the point of being obnoxious. What I mean by that is every time you log into your account a chat window opens up and one of their support people asks if you need any help. I find it to be a little too much, but newer users may not.

A note about emails that you get with any of these searches. While both InfoUSA and Infofree, as well as many list brokers, offer email addresses with their lists, that doesn't mean you can load them into your auto responder and start sending emails. To remain compliant with the CAN-Spam act, any list broker can only offer you email address that have opted in to some offer they have made in the past. The broker will be willing to take the email you create and then send it to the list you request, but they will not give you a list of email addresses to send to yourself. Obviously anyone on their list that accepts your offer and opts in to your list can now be remarked by you.

4. Leads Companies. Just like with list brokers, if you do a Google search for Leads Companies you will find many of them. Like a list broker, a leads company will take your search criteria and pull potential customers together in a list for you. Some you might check into are:

- ✓ directmailtools.com
- ✓ usadata.com,
- ✓ insidesales.com,
- ✓ leadfeed.com

I have not personally used any of these, but know others who have had good success with them.

5. Other sources. There are many data directories available, both online and off. A trip to your local library will give you access to ReferenceUSA, the North American Industry Classification System (NAICS.com) and the Standard Industrial Classification Manual. These resource tools will help you identify exact categories of businesses that will be good prospects for you, making working with your list broker or online list source easier. NAICS.com also offers a list service you can check out.

There are several online service that collect small business data and post it. One is www.Manta.com. Another is yellowpages.com. The challenge with many of these online sources is that they are dependent on the business owner actually going online and "claiming" their listing, then making certain the data is correct. Ask yourself this question: "Have I updated my Manta.com listing?" For the listings that have been claimed, the data is accurate. The question is always how many owners in your target market have completed their profile?

Voice Broadcasting

I have mentioned using this technique as a way of expediting your prospecting to business owners. This is an easy process. First you upload a list of phone numbers you want contacted from an Excel spreadsheet. Then record the message you want delivered, talk for a few seconds or a couple of minutes, your choice. You can control what time of day you want the messages sent and whether you want voicemails left.

How would you use this? Take the email script I gave you earlier, shorten it to just three of four sentences emphasizing that you are a business owner looking to joint venture a marketing campaign with another non-competing business owner. Tell them the target market and the results you expect. Invite them to call you for more information. Give your telephone number two times. You should be able to record that in 20 to 30 seconds.

The advantage of this is you can send your message to several hundred prospects in just a few minutes for very little money. My personal experience with this type of marketing is that many times the person will not listen to their message but see that they missed a call. So they just do *69 and call back, interrupting me at a time when it might not be convenient for me to talk.

Here's how I handle this potential problem. I set up the source number, that is, the number that shows up in the recipients caller ID with a voice mail and record the exact same message. What that means is when someone answers my call they get the message I've recorded, but if they don't and just do a *69 they still hear my message. The company you use as your voice broadcasting platform can help you create this structure. Be aware that they may require you to use one of their numbers and add a small fee to your monthly bill for this service. It's worth it!

Some companies you might checkout are:

- ✓ callfire.com
- ✓ voiceshot.com
- ✓ onecallnow.com

CHAPTER EIGHT

DESIGNING YOUR ADS
AND POSTCARD LAYOUT

I have mentioned several times that this is far simpler than you might think. That is based on my personal experience as well as observing clients who implement the Capture Your Neighborhood Formula. Here's my recommendations for streamlining this phase of the program.

First, find a graphics person. If you want to do this with a local person, so that you can meet with them face to face, there are a couple of things you can do. Craigs List is a great place to find someone looking to freelance as a graphic artist. If you work with them to design a basic template, then it becomes an easy matter to plug in ads for future campaigns. Another place to look is the local university or community college art department. If you don't have one nearby, contact the art teacher at the nearest high school. Students are always looking for "real world" work experience, and a project they can add to their portfolio is a welcome opportunity.

If you're comfortable working with someone online and don't care where they live, then here are three sources to look into: odesk.com, warriorforum.com (warriors for hire section) and fiverr.com. My personal favorite is fiverr.com. Here's how it works.

Go to the site and create an account. You will need a Paypal account as well, as that is how you pay for your "gigs." On the site you'll find quite a few categories of services being offered, or you can type a search term into the search bar. If you enter "graphic design" you'll find many artists from literally all over the world who are willing to do your project for $5 US. That's correct...$5! Some may ask for an additional 'gig' (another $5) to give you a specific file type for the finished product, or to do the job in an expedited time frame. But for the most part you can get a job done for just $5.

Once you choose someone and pay for the service, the fiverr.com system will send you an email asking you to provide information about exactly what you want. Here you can upload files and be very specific about your requirements, or you can ask the artist to use their creativity on your project. Once the artist delivers your work and you approve it, then fiverr pays the artist. If they do not deliver within the time period they have promised you have the option to cancel the gig, get your money back, and choose another artist.

I have done close to 100 projects using fiverr people (the cover of this book was done using a fiverr artist in Israel). In all of that time I have only had two negative experiences, and in both cases got my money refunded and found another person to do the job. I encourage you to check out fiverr.com. Just realize that you will get sucked in looking at all of the crazy things people are willing to do for $5!

Design Specifications for Printing Postcards

Whether you decide to take your artwork to a local printer and manage the postcard production in a more personal way, or upload your "camera ready" art to an online company who prints and mails your cards for you, there are important design specifications you need to adhere to.

These are:

- Resolution: no less than 300 dpi
- Color Space: CMYK
- Safety Zone: 1/8" inside
- Bleed: 1/8" outside

If you're not familiar with these terms, don't worry. Your graphics person will be. Your local printer can probably provide you with a template showing exactly what they'll need, and the online companies you might use will certainly have this. Just give the template to your artist and they'll know what to do.

Online Printing and Mailing Service Companies

Twenty years ago when I first began experimenting with what has become the Capture Your Neighborhood Formula the internet didn't exist--or at least not in a way that was accessible by the average business person. Today the world of marketing and advertising is totally different, and the primary cause of that transformation is the world wide web. Now you can "outsource" almost every step in the CYN Formula, and do so in a cost efficient way.

Perhaps the best innovation in the last couple of years for this type of marketing are the internet based companies who offer "full service" printing and mailing. Now you can upload your artwork and mailing list to their site. They will then print your postcards, sort, stamp and mail them all from their warehouse. You don't have to touch a thing! In many cases they will do this in the same price range, less than 70 cents a card, that is the target for the CYN Formula. If you are doing a saturation mailing using EDDM then you can absolutely have everything done for you and stay within this budget.

You'll have to do your own analysis, but the way I am teaching this to my own clients is that even if I have to pay a few cents apiece for my own ad going out, if I can minimize my time involved in managing, then it is worth it to incur a modest cost for the campaign. Use the tools we now have available: from voice broadcasting to highly focused list acquisition, automated email invitations, graphic design from fiverr, and companies who will take over all the printing and mailing steps. All the of time consuming work that you as a business owner used to do, at least for the first few campaigns, can now be outsourced. That means that your primary responsibility for creating a successful campaign is to have enough telephone conversations with other business owners to find two partners. And after you do a few campaigns, most of them will be coming back to you asking when they can participate again.

Here are some companies that I am familiar with that you should analyze. There are certainly more companies who offer this service, I just don't have experience with them. I suggest you will want to analyze them yourself because their offers change over time. What was the best deal last month may not be today. All of these companies have customer service people who will help with your questions and can guide you through the process. This is really valuable as you are starting out with the CYN Formula.

- ✓ www.gotprint.net
- ✓ www.expresscopy.com
- ✓ www.psprint.com
- ✓ www.overnightprints.com
- ✓ www.everydoordirectmailusa.com

These companies will also be willing to send you a sample pack of the various sizes of cards they print. This will give you a good example to show to prospective partners. The card they send will only feature one company where you are going to have three on your cards, but it will show other business owners how much space there is to work with. Each company also has a series of templates you can download and give to your graphic design person. This way you are uploading exactly what they need to complete your job quickly.

Variations of Card Layout

I have experimented with different ad layouts over the years. Obviously you can sell and design your own program, but here is what I have learned.

1. Still the absolute best layout for the three businesses on the card is to print the card in a landscape orientation and divide the card into three equal sections, front and back. What I typically suggest to the other advertisers, and always do myself, is put a compelling headline and brief copy on the front, then an offer on the back side. I like to put a coupon on the card, or a code that must be used to get the benefit of the offer. This provides good tracking so your partners can see the return on investment from the campaign.

The back side of the card is required to have a space for the address. The size depends on the type of postage you will be using. I always put the address space in my companies section of the back of the card. It makes the other participants feel like I've given them full value for their money. This is the only way I teach my consulting clients to do the CYN Formula.

2. I've tried just one partner and given them the entire front of the card, while I use the back for my advertisement. The

first negative is that I now have to underwrite a larger portion of the cost of the campaign. The extra space, and copy that I can add, has not resulted in an improvement in ROI over the layout I described above.

3. Another layout is to give one partner advertiser the option to pay extra and buy the entire back side of the postcard, while the other partner and my company split the front side. Again, there has not been an appreciable increase in ROI for any of us with this method. I have also found that fewer of the participants in this format want to join on another mailing in the future.

CHAPTER NINE

COPYWRITING FOR CYN POSTCARDS

If there is a "value add" that you can offer to your joint venture partners it is helping them compose their ads. Most business owners assume that an ad should be like what the Yellow Pages sales person wants them to do. That is, use their company name as the headline, a catchy slogan or photo, their phone number, and some platitude about "we're the best!"

Really? Think about it. When you see an advertisement like that do you ever stop and read it? I mean actually read all the copy and think to yourself, "hmmm, maybe I should call them." Almost never! Why? Because the ad doesn't say anything about what the potential customer is interested in-- their 'hot buttons.' The ad is all about the company and nothing about the prospect.

When I work with a client to help them enhance their marketing there are several exercises I ask them to complete. While a detailed explanation of each of these is beyond the scope of this report, let me give you a quick overview designed to help make you a better advertising copy writer.

Effective copy speaks to the needs of the potential customer--it is focused on the conversation in their mind about your product or service. Your prospect doesn't care if you've been in business since 1876 and have the greatest group of employees since George Washington picked his first Cabinet. All a prospect cares about is having their personal needs met. If you can demonstrate your ability to do that in your advertising, then you have a chance to capture their attention and eventually their business.

So how do you do that?

One of the first activities I do with a client is a process that we call **Customer Discovery Questions**. This exercise is based on the belief that "If you want to know what John Smith buys, you have to see the world through John Smith's eyes." That is, until you understand what is important to your customer, you can't write effective advertising copy. We go through a series of 14 Customer Discovery Questions, let me stimulate your thinking with just four of them:

1. Under what circumstances does the typical prospect start to think about buying what you sell?

2. What things are important to your prospect when buying what you sell? Consider both the product or service itself, AND the buying process. Think about what prospects want AND what they want to avoid.

3. What are the relevant and important issues that a prospect needs to be aware of when making a decision about what you sell?

4. What do YOU do to give the customer what he or she wants?

Many times when we begin this exercise, it is the first time our client has actually stopped and thought about what might be important to their customer. It can be a very revealing experience! Most of us as business owners are so focused on what we offer that we rarely stop and think about how a prospective client views or experiences our company and our team. It can be sobering to realize how much money we have left on the table over the time we've been in business because of this ignorance.

The second concept I want to share with you is what we call **The Marketing Equation**. This idea is based on the belief that marketing is science, not art. That by understanding more about our customer, "seeing the world through their eyes," we can craft our advertising statements to speak to the conversation in their minds and win the right to talk further with them.

The Marketing Equation has four components. As I describe them, I want you to think about an advertisement you will be writing for your business. It could be a flyer, newspaper ad, the homepage of your website, or the ad you are going to put on a CYN Formula postcard. I want you to begin to lay out each and every marketing piece you create for your business using this formula. Here are the components:

1. Interrupt--getting qualified prospects to pay attention to your marketing. Think of this as the headline for your ad. It must be based on the hot buttons that are important to your prospect. It should answer one or more of the Discovery Questions you thought through earlier. Here are some hints:

- ✓ Your company name is not a hot button headline for your prospect. DO NOT put it at the top of your advertisements.
- ✓ No "False Betas." A false beta is an interrupt that has no relevance to your company or product. For example, putting a woman in a bikini in your ad when you are in the sandwich deli business. While you will catch the eye of many people looking at your ad, once

they realize the image has no congruence with your product or service they will move on and never read the rest of your ad.

✓ A question can be a good interrupt, but it is difficult to phrase in broad enough terms to interrupt a large cross section of the readership. It is better to make a declarative statement.

2. Engage--think of this as a sub-headline. What you are saying to your reader is that "if you continue to read, there is information coming that will help in your decision making process about my product or service."

3. Educate--identify important issues for the prospect and demonstrate how you solve them. For a postcard campaign bullet points are a great way to do this.

4. Offer--give them a low risk way to take the next step in the buying process. You want to make your prospect feel like they're in charge. The next step may be coming into your place of business, but it could also be requesting a report or visiting a web page. Too often we try to jump from first meeting a prospect to handing them a contract and asking for their signature. Like when you were dating, the sales process requires a time of wooing. This is particularly true if you offer a product or service that is specialized, expensive, or in a highly competitive marketplace.

Let me give just one example of how this works in a "real world" setting--writing an advertisement to go on a postcard. I'll make this really generic so you can visualize a variety of companies using the format.

1. Interrupt: On the front side of the card I'd have a full color image that is relevant to the company product/service. Over

the top of the photo is this Interrupt (headline):

3 Critical Characteristics to Demand From Your
_____ (fill in the service provided by the company. For example: attorney, kids dentist, kitchen cabinets, carpet cleaner, etc.)

2. The "Engage" portion, or sub headline. How about something like:

Does Yours Stack Up?

OK, with just those few words you have the attention of anyone who has been thinking about the product or service you offer. We still haven't told them the name of our company, or any of the great slogans we've come up with that describe how wonderful we are. But you know what? Right now they are turning over the postcard to learn more...and that's the whole point! Let's keep going.

3. Educate. What are those 3 Critical Characteristics? Here is where we tell them. And because we only have part of a postcard to do so, bullet points are the logical way to do it. What do we put in the bullet points? We speak directly to the issues in the mind of the prospect we identified in the Discovery Questions exercise. For example

- ✓ Expertise. (Make a few word statement about the level of experience and excellence a prospect should expect. Obviously you can meet this criteria).
- ✓ Value. (Here is where you briefly address their concern about cost of the service or product).
- ✓ Customer Experience. (What you do to make the customer feel comfortable shopping with you.

4. Offer. Now you put your company name and tell them the

specific next step you want them to take.

XYZ Company. Go to www.xyzreport.com to get your free report and see how We Stack Up.

OK, obviously those exact terms won't work for all situations. The point was to help you think through how an ad that actually addresses the needs of your prospects should be structured. When you stop and think about it, it is easier to structure an ad like this than to try and cram in a lot of generalities and platitudes that really don't tell your prospect anything.

If you can help your CYN Formula partners with this, they will come back to you over and over for more postcard campaigns. Why? Because they work! If you are interested in learning more about the Marketing Equation please visit my website at www.GordonVanWechel.com. There is a page called the Video Vault that has marketing strategy training programs you can review, including a ten minute video description of the Marketing Equation.

CHAPTER TEN

IMPLEMENTING CYN WITHOUT GETTING OVERWHELMED

As small business owners we are constantly fighting overwhelm. You know what that is...way too much to do and not nearly enough hours in the day to get it all done. I would be doing you a real disservice if I gave you a powerful strategy like CYN and didn't also share a plan for translating the idea into action. The Capture Your Neighborhood Formula will be a complete waste for you if all you do now that you've read it is throw it onto one of the piles on your desk and plan to "get around to it."

Based on my experience working with many busy business owners, here is a plan to implement CYN.

Day One: 30 minutes. Identify two or three specific target groups to market to. These might be other businesses, consumers, or both. Write down a detailed profile of the target group.

Day Two: 30 minutes. Think about categories of other business owners who would like to market to this same group of prospects. Write down the categories. Using the internet, identify at least five companies in your area for each of these categories.

60 minutes. Have a staff member compile a spreadsheet with name, address, phone, and email information for each of the companies you identified. As an alternative, you can use one of the data companies I mentioned earlier.

Day Three: 60 minutes. Research several of the online providers I mentioned, or others you find. What is their current offer for postcard printing and mailing? Can you use the EDDM program? Your objective is to determine the cost of the mailing so you can properly present the offer to potential partners.

If you have the time, you can also check out local printers and mail houses and compare the costs with the online companies. Maybe it will be better for you to manage this project "in house."

Day Four: 60 minutes. Contact potential JV partners. I like to use email, phone blast, even putting a message on their business Facebook page if you can find it, rather than a cold telephone call. This is "pull" marketing rather than "push," and keeps you in more of the authority position. However, many times I've just picked up the phone and called other business owners. Remember, you're not a salesperson hoping for a deal, you're a fellow business owner offering them a great opportunity to find new prospects and customers. So do whatever is the most comfortable for you. If you belong to a leads group, service club, or Chamber of Commerce you have an immediate pool of potential partners!

Day Five: 60 minutes. Repeat Day Four, if necessary. Using the scripts I gave you, it should be a fairly quick process to find two partners. They may want to see a sample of the card, or talk further about exactly where you are mailing if you're doing a saturation campaign, but once they grasp the concept you are proposing, they will either make a yes or no decision quite quickly.

Day Six: 60 minutes. Get logo, artwork, ad copy from

partners, and do your own. This may take several days to assemble and require multiple phone calls, but should be little more than an hour of your time in total. Once you have all the information assembled, send it to the graphics person you have engaged to create the postcard.

Day Seven: 45 minutes. Proof the artwork. If it is complete, get a copy to each of your partners. Once they have signed off, upload to your local printers website or send to the online company you have selected. If you have selected a full service printer and mailing house, you are done.

Day Eight: 60 to 90 minutes. If you have chosen to manage the mailing yourself, making sure it is correctly sorted and getting it to the post office is your final step.

When you add all the time up, you're somewhere in the eight to nine hours of actual hands on work for you. Now I've done this many times, and you would be justified in saying to yourself, "well I can't get it done that fast." So let's say it takes you at least 50% longer, maybe 15 hours over a two week period of time to get your first Capture Your Neighborhood Formula campaign completed.

That's an average of one hour a day. Let's say your mailing is only 2500 pieces, and your partners have paid for all of the hard costs. At a 2% response rate, you'll have 50 new potential customers to talk with. Is that worth 15 hours of your time?

The second campaign you'll be faster...and you will have learned which steps can be delegated to someone else. So maybe now you only spend 8 hours to get the same 50 potential customers. The leverage is getting better!

By the time you've done four or five of these campaigns, your personal hands on time can be minimized, you will have trained someone to do much of the fulfillment work. Even more important, the marketing partners you have worked with in the first campaigns are ready to do another. So your prospecting time and cost is less. And they've been sharing their experience with business owners they know, who also want to get into the mailing co-op.

I hope you're seeing what the Capture Your Neighborhood Formula can do to help you grow your business. Now, go make it happen.

ABOUT THE AUTHOR

Gordon Van Wechel is a serial entrepreneur who created three national companies in three different industries. For the past eleven years he has consulted with dozens of business owners helping them develop marketing strategies for business growth.

Gordon is the President of The Alchemy Consulting Group. He currently lives in Albuquerque, NM

Gordon Van Wechel

The 11 Most Asked Questions About Working With The Alchemy Consulting Group

(and 11 great reasons why you'll jump at the chance to get your business rocketing forward.)

1. So Who is The Alchemy Consulting Group?

Alchemy is a strategic marketing and business growth consulting firm started in 2010 by Jennine Michael and Gordon Van Wechel. It is an outgrowth of a consulting practice that Gordon first began in 2003. Between them, Jennine and Gordon have over 60 years of hands on experience as entrepreneurs, building and selling several businesses of their own. The same is true of all of our associate consultants, who are experienced business owners. That means we know what it's like to work 80 hours a week and "wear all the hats" in the business.

Unlike most ad agencies or more traditional consulting firms, Alchemy has created a menu of services, we call them "modules." These have been designed to provide our clients with specific solutions to their business growth challenges regardless of how long you might have been in business. Whether you are the owner of a new business just starting out, or have an established company looking to expand, we can offer tools and strategies to help you take the next step. The benefit to you is that we don't expect you to fit into our "marketing mold." We will be able to help you evaluate exactly what you need, and can afford, at this time in your business.

2. Why Do I Even Need a Consultant?

Every great sports star, business person, and superstar is surrounded by coaches and advisors. As the world of business moves faster and gets more competitive, it can be difficult to keep up with the changes in your industry as well as the innovations in marketing and management. Having a business growth consultant is no longer a luxury; it's become a necessity.

If you're honest, you know that it is almost impossible to get an objective answer from yourself. That is not to say that you cannot survive in business without a consultant, but it's almost impossible to thrive.

A consultant can see the forest for the trees. A consultant will make you focus on the game, making you run more laps than you feel like. A consultant will tell it like it really is. A consultant will give you small pointers. A consultant will listen, and understand your pain. A consultant will help you remember the dreams you had when going into business…and help you get back on track to achieving them.

3. OK, so What is the First Step?

We'll ask you to complete our Marketing Audit. This is a series of questions, most of them are simple Yes/No answers, but there are several questions that will require a more detailed response. The purpose of the audit is to help you pinpoint areas of strength in your marketing now, and help identify those aspects of your plan that could use further work. A common experience of people participating in this exercise is a lot of ideas and excitement about what can be done to bring in more customers and profits. It will also prompt some questions about specific marketing tactics and how to implement them.

Once you have returned your audit, we'll schedule a time to meet together. This typically is a 60 to 90 minute conversation where we help you dig deeper into the level your company is performing at today, and where you'd like it to be in twelve months. It is also an opportunity for you to get to know us a little more, and see if working together makes sense. At the end of this meeting, at your request, we will prepare a proposal detailing our recommendations specific to your company, and the investment you will be making. You can then decide when you'd like to begin.

There is no charge for this initial meeting.

4. What Will You Do, and How Long Will it Take?

Just as every person is different, we believe each business is different. The plan that we suggest for your business will be based on the evaluation we make after reviewing your Marketing Audit and the conversation we have in the initial meeting. Which is to say that I cannot give you a specific idea of what we will do in your business, because we haven't designed your plan yet.

I can tell you that while about 80% of our strategic marketing focus today is online, we still incorporate traditional offline tools like direct mail and telephone marketing. We do that because they work. The particular mix of strategies for your company will depend on your goals, current situation, budget, competitive landscape, and personnel available to handle an influx of new customers.

Here's something else. Part of the Marketing Audit considers your current capacity. That is, how much more business can you handle well? It is no value to your business suddenly bring in 100 new clients when you only have the staff to properly serve 15 of them.   We call this evaluating the "inside reality" of your company and is included in our modules.

As far as how long a typical program might take, we like to make commitments in 12 month increments. We don't try to lock someone in a contract saying that, but the plan we design for you will be based on a year of implementation.

If you've been in business for more than a few months you've already seen, and maybe even purchased, one or more so called "quick fixes." Most consultants want you to believe that they can solve your business growth problems in a few days. Our philosophy at Alchemy is that establishing a foundation for long term success in your business means not just scraping the surface with a few "Google secrets." We prefer to design a multi-channel marketing strategy that offers you controlled growth. That means implementing one or two modules initially, then, as they pay for themselves, adding more marketing. Over the course of a year, working together, we help you fully capitalize on current markets for your product/service, and extend the reach of your company into new areas.

5. How Do You Know This Will Work in My Industry?

Really simple. Our team of consultants are experts in sales, marketing, business development, management strategies, hiring key people, and evaluation of markets; just to name a few of their competencies. With more than 250 business building tactics in our arsenal you will quickly see how effective and powerful our modules are.

Add to this the fact that we have consulted with more than

300 companies in over 50 business categories and you can see that very likely that we have worked in a business that is the same or very similar to yours.

6. How Much Time and Money will This Cost Me?

The first couple of months your involvement in the processes will require more time. That might be review of copy or collateral materials, training your team in a new sales system, or regularly scheduled update meetings you'll have with one of our team members. The actual implementation of tactics, what we call the "back office fulfillment" duties, are all done by one of our groups of specialists. If part of your program calls for a revision of your website, the actual work will be done by our web builders. If you are doing a Real Time Bidding program, then another of our teams will handle the day to day details of that marketing channel for you.

As to the financial investment…well, nothing! That is if you look at it from the same perspective as we do. That's the difference between a cost and an investment. Everything we propose for your company is a true investment in your future. Not only will you create great results in your business, but you'll learn more than just marketing strategies. Working with our consultants will give you an education from experienced entrepreneurs you could never get in school, and this is knowledge that you can repeat over and over.

So you don't think I'm dodging the question, let me give you a range. We have clients who invest as little as $500 monthly and others who spend $10,000 a month. It will depend on your company, budget, short and long term growth goals, and how aggressively you want to pursue them.

7. Are There Any Guarantees?

In a word, no. We will never promise any specific result, nor can we guarantee that any of your goals will become a reality. The bottom line is we are your consultants, but it is still your business and it's up to you and your team to take the sales opportunities we bring you and convert those prospects to customers and eventually to raving fans of your business.

Only *you* can be fully accountable for your success. We guarantee to give you the best service we can, the benefit of all our experience and proven business growth strategies, and to encourage and even cajole you to reach for your goals. But at the end of the day it is your business.

8. You're Based in Another City, How Does That Work?

You may have read Thomas Friedman's book from a few years ago called "The World Is Flat." His point was that with the communication tools available today business has truly become international. Even the shoe store down the street can have an ecommerce website or a store on eBay and sell to the whole world. Our business is living proof of that new reality: 80% of our clients live in another state. We regularly supply them with reports and updates via email, and schedule progress review conversations using phone or Skype.

Occasionally a client will want us to be at their location for a specific purpose, but generally that is an expense that you don't need to incur.

9. Do You Just Help With My Marketing?

While our primary focus is on marketing and business

growth strategies, we'll help you in other areas too. For example, part of our Reputation Marketing module includes a training program helping your staff become more adept at customer service. I mentioned earlier the concept of the "inside reality" of your company, we'll help you identify operations within your business that can be improved.

We strongly believe in systems, the more you can implement systems in your business the better you can run your business instead of having it run you!

10. When is The Best Time to Get Started?

Yesterday. Really.

OK, right now, today; before you take another marketing step, waste another dollar, lose another sale, work another 70 hour week.

Far too many business people wait and see. They confuse activity with accomplishment and think that working harder will make it all better. Remember, what you know got you to where you are. To get to where you want to go you've got to make some changes and most likely learn something new.

There is no time like the present to get started on your dreams and goals.

11. How Do I Start?

Call us toll free at 877-978-2110 and ask for a Marketing Audit. You'll be connected with one of our consultants who will help you get started. We'll set up a time for an interview so we can learn about your business. Then we'll work with you to create a plan that helps you achieve your goals on a timeline that is affordable and makes sense for your business.

This may seem like a big job at the beginning, but with an Alchemy Consultant you'll have someone guiding you each step of the way.

Could You Profit From A Free, One Hour Flash Consultation Focused On Your Business?

I want to thank you for buying this book, and if you've found this page it means you probably even read most of it. The Capture Your Neighborhood Formula is just one of more than 250 business growth tactics we consider when working with our clients.

Would you like to know some other ways to grow your business?

I'd like to offer you a free, one hour "flash consulting" session. What that means is a very quick, 10,000 foot view of your company and current marketing efforts. We'll ask a lot of questions, and answer yours. We might point you in a new direction, suggest a strategy that you hadn't considered, or help you look at what you're now doing in a new light.

This is a conversation about marketing and your business...it is not a thinly disguised pitch for you to hire us. Never once have I had anyone say it wasn't worth their time!

To take advantage of this offer you have to do a couple of things:

1. go to www.TheAlchemyConsultingGroup.com/flashconsult

2. answer the questions and give us your contact info

3. we'll call and schedule an hour that works for both of us to meet by telephone

4. come to our meeting with an open mind, a pen and pad ready to take notes, and be in a quiet place where you will not be interrupted.

I look forward to talking with you.

Gordon